LET'S PLAY RHYTHM

BRUCE GERTZ

MW00446858

BRUCE GERTZ

LET'S PLAY RHYTHM

Variations on Rhythm Changes for the Study of Improvisation,
Ear Training and Composition

© 2005 by advance music
All Rights Reserved
No part of this publication may be reproduced,
stored in retrieval system, or transmitted, in any form or by any means,
electronic, mechanical, photocopying, recording, or otherwise,
without prior permission of advance music.
International Copyright Secured.

All compositions © 2005 Bruce Gertz Music, A.S.C.A.P

Photographs © 2005 Nicole Goodhue

Recording
PBS Studios Westwood, MA. USA
Peter Kontrimas, Engineer

Additional Recording
Bruce Gertz

Music typesetting and layout
Hans-Jörg Rüdiger

Published by
advance music
D-72108 Rottenburg N.
Germany
www.advancemusic.com

Production:
Veronika Gruber

Printed in Germany

ISBN 3-89221-068-3

An intelligently written, clear and concise book that can be used by players of all instruments. With Bruce's clever lines (and titles!) anyone will come away with a more complete and facile understanding of rhythm changes!

Bill Mays

Let's Play Rhythm, the new book by Bruce Gertz, is a must for all players who wish to get to the core and a deeper, functional use of the jazz vocabulary. We as players and teachers speak of the importance of "RHYTHM CHANGES," but Bruce Gertz has put these concepts into one concise book that is absolutely great. Bruce Gertz is a seasoned player and teacher who has left no stone unturned, melodically, nor rhythmically, for the aspiring player, no matter what instrument. He has truly saturated ways one can approach and negotiate the sound of the essential "meat and potatoes" forms of jazz, "RHYTHM CHANGES." This form itself is not new, but Bruce Gertz's concepts and tunes are fresh, extremely clear to understand and, most importantly, he has made them fun to play while learning the "real deal!" This is no easy task! BRAVO AND CONGRATULATIONS!

Rufus Reid, Bassist

Bruce Gertz's new project about rhythm changes is excellent. There is enough material there to generate a one or two semester lab here at Berklee, where both of us teach. The quality of the CDs alone is worth the price of admission!! And in addition to all the rhythm changes material, there is also some great stuff that's more about the "tools" of improvising ... Highly recommended!!!

Mick Goodrick

Bruce has put together a very comprehensive package for musicians that are serious about improving. It can apply to all instruments and it's informative, smart and entertaining as well. Check it out!!

Antonio Sanchez

What a great premise Bruce Gertz puts forth: use the old warhorse of rhythm changes (which is required reading for all jazz students) as the framework to develop all sorts of improvisational approaches, of course applicable in many other situations. What I like about this book is that with the help of the CD (featuring a great band by the way) and written out examples, a student can get right to the point and get immediate results.

David Liebman

TABLE OF CONTENTS

Track lists: Discs 1, 2 and 3 8
Foreword, Acknowledgements, Dedication .11

INTRODUCTION

Applications 13
How to use the play-along 15
The AABA Form 17

PART I BASS LINES

Bass lines 21
Where the passing tones come from 22
Quick reference chart: chord tones – passing tones 23
Variations of melodic bass lines over I VI II V four measure phrase . . .24

Disc 1 Bass Lines
Bass line 1a, 2 feel 26
Bass line 1b 27
Transcribe third chorus 28
Bass line 1c 29
Transcribe second chorus 30
Bass line 2 31
Bass line 3 32
Bass line 4 33
Bass line 5 34
Bass line 6 35
Bass line 7 36
Bass line 8 37
Bass line 9 38
Bass line 10 39
Bass line 11 40
Reharmonization 1 41
Reharmonization 2 42
Reharmonization 3 43
Reharmonization 4 44
Reharmonization 5 45
Reharmonization 6 46
Reharmonization 7 (transcription exercise) 47
Reharmonization 8 48
Reharmonization 9 (transcription exercise) 49
Bass line 3, key of C 50
Reharmonization 1, key of C 51
Reharmonization 10, key of F 52
Bass line 9, key of F 53
Bass line 11a, key of F 54
Transcribe bass part 6/4 key of F 55
Transcribe bass part Mambo, key of E♭ 56
Bass Line 1c, key of A♭ 57
Bass line 11a, key of A♭ 58
Bass line 4, key of D♭ 59
Bass line 9, key of G 60
Bass line 11a, key of G 61
Bass line 4, key of A 62

Bass line 12, key of A 63
Bass line 13, key of D 64
Bass line 14, key of D 65
Open changes 1 (transcription exercise) 66
Open changes 2, key of F (transcription exercise) 67
Variation, key of G (transcription exercise) 68
Free Style 1 (transcription exercise) 69
Free Style 2 (transcription exercise) 70
Suggested listening 71

PART II PLAY-ALONG

Diatonic Melodies 73
Major and minor scales and modes 74
Hop on the Scale 82
Peaceful Resolution 84
Chin Up 86
Red Star 88
Snake Shoes 90
Broiled 92

Rhythmic Melodies 95
The Rhythm Method 96
Kicks 98
Car Horns (part 1 & 2) 100
Hit Me 104
Don't Pick it Up 106

Pentatonic and Blues Scale Melodies .109
Basic pentatonic scales 110
Pentatonic exercises 112
Penta-Rhythm 114
Pentup Bop 116
You First 118
Not Yet 120
Riff Off 122
Penta Roll 124
Overweight and Underpaid 126

Diminished Melodies and Upper Structure Triads 129
Diminished scales 130
Upper structure triads 135
I'm Thinking 140
The Lizard of Odds 142
Rhythm a dim 144
Stress Test (part 1 & 2) 146
Ring Around Uranus 150
Dirty Details 152
Horse Power 154
Tumbling 156

Intervalic Melodies 159
Intervalic lines 160
Quarts and Fifths 162
Red Note Special 164

ABOUT THE AUTHOR 166

DISC 1

Play-along – rhythm section only

Left channel: piano & drums
Right channel: bass & drums

Bruce Gertz – Bass
Russell Hoffman – Piano
Robert Kaufman – Drums
Jerry Bergonzi – Drums on tracks 33 and 34

1	Tuning note A	0:22
2	Bass line approach examples	
	1–10 (I VI II V progression), slow tempo	2:44
3	Bass line examples 1–10, medium tempo	1:38
4	"2 Feel" bass line 1a & 1b, medium bounce	3:05
5	Bass line 1c, medium-up	1:49
6	Bass line 2, medium	1:55
7	Bass lines 3, 4, 5, medium	2:24
8	Bass lines 6, 7, 8, slow	3:50
9	Bass lines 9, 10, 11, medium	3:27
10	Reharmonization 1, medium	2:56
11	Reharmonization 2, medium-up, ♩=205	2:05
12	Reharmonization 3, medium-up, ♩=192	2:08
13	Reharmonization 4, medium-up, ♩=202	2:02
14	Reharmonization 5, medium-up, ♩=180	2:15
15	Reharmonization 6, medium funk, B♭ pedal, swing bridge	2:00
16	Reharmonization 7, up tempo, dominant pedal, swing bridge	2:00
17	Reharmonization 8, medium swing, ♩=110	2:41
18	Reharmonization 9, up swing, ♩=216	1:30
19	Key of C, bass line 3, ♩=176	1:50
20	Key of C, Reharmonization 1, ♩=172	1:45
21	Key of F, Bossa, ♩=126	2:22
22	Key of F, bass lines 9 & 11a, ♩=200	1:35
23	Key of F, 6/4 time, ♩=200	1:26
24	Key of E♭, Mambo, ♩=168	1:50
25	Key of A♭, bass lines 1c & 11a, ♩=240	2:00
26	Key of D♭, bass line 4 & chords #1, ♩=146	2:08
27	Key of G, bass lines 9 & 11a, ♩=192	2:08
28	Key of A, bass lines 4 & 12, ♩=138	2:18
29	Key of D, bass lines 13 & 14, ♩=140	2:12
30	Key of B♭, Open Changes 1, ♩=264	3:15
31	Key of F, Open Changes 2, ♩=182	3:07
32	Key of G, Variation 1, ♩=198	2:49
33	Key of B♭, free style, ♩=150	2:45
34	Key of B♭, free style, ♩=208	2:45

DISC 2

Play-along – rhythm section and melodies

Bruce Gertz – Bass
Russell Hoffman – Piano
Robert Kaufman – Drums

1	Tuning Note A	0:21
2	Hop On The Scale	1:44 *
3	Peaceful Resolution	3:24 *
4	Chin Up	1:50 *
5	Red Star	2:22 †
6	Snake Shoes	2:18 *
7	Broiled	2:23 °
8	The Rhythm Method	2:04 *
9	Kicks	2:21 *
10	Car Horns	3:11 ‡
11	Hit Me	1:27 *
12	Don't Pick It Up	1:46 *
13	Penta-Rhythm	2:03 *
14	Pentup Bop	3:26 °
15	You First	2:13 ‡
16	Not Yet	3:25 °
17	Riff Off	2:01 ‡
18	Penta Roll	2:03 °
19	Overweight and Underpaid	2:38 †‡
20	I'm Thinking	2:00 °
21	The Lizard of Odds (slow)	2:58 *
22	The Lizard of Odds (fast)	2:46 *
23	Rhythm a Dim	1:57 †
24	Stress Test	3:07 *
25	Ring Around Uranus	1:43 †
26	Dirty Details	2:00 °
27	Dirty Details F pedal	1:55 °
28	Horse Power	2:34 *
29	Tumbling	2:00 °
30	Quarts & Fifths	2:04 *
31	Red Note Special	3:00 *

all compositions by Bruce Gertz

* *Jerry Bergonzi – tenor saxophone, drums on The Lizard of Odds*
† *Ken Cervenka – trumpet*
‡ *Jeff Galindo – trombone*
° *Matt Marvuglio – Flute*

DISC 3

Listening version

Bruce Gertz – Bass
Russell Hoffman – Piano
Robert Kaufman – Drums

1	Tuning Note A	0:21
2	Hop On The Scale	1:44 *
3	Peaceful Resolution	3:24 *
4	Chin Up	1:50 *
5	Red Star	2:22 †
6	Snake Shoes	2:18 *
7	Broiled	2:23 °
8	The Rhythm Method	2:04 *
9	Kicks	2:21 *
10	Car Horns	3:11 ‡
11	Hit Me	1:27 *
12	Don't Pick It Up	1:46 *
13	Penta-Rhythm	2:03 *
14	Pentup Bop	3:26 °
15	You First	2:13 ‡
16	Not Yet	3:25 °
17	Riff Off	2:01 ‡
18	Penta Roll	2:03 °
19	Overweight and Underpaid	2:38 †‡
20	I'm Thinking	2:00 °
21	The Lizard of Odds (slow)	2:58 *
22	The Lizard of Odds (fast)	2:46 *
23	Rhythm a Dim	1:57 †
24	Stress Test	3:07 *
25	Ring Around Uranus	1:43 †
26	Dirty Details	2:00 °
27	Dirty Details F pedal	1:55 °
28	Horse Power	2:34 *
29	Tumbling	2:00 °
30	Quarts & Fifths	2:04 *
31	Red Note Special	3:00 *

all compositions by Bruce Gertz

*   *Jerry Bergonzi – tenor saxophone, drums on The Lizard of Odds*
†   *Ken Cervenka – trumpet*
‡   *Jeff Galindo – trombone*
°   *Matt Marvuglio – Flute*

FOREWORD

Over the course of my teaching career which began in 1975 I have learned a great deal about the learning process. For most musicians and all people it is through repetition that they are able to internalize their language. Once a student really knows a song (melody, harmony and rhythm) it then becomes possible for them to improvise and try variations of ideas over that song. It does however take some effort and dedication to the song before really hearing it. If you are learning lines to a play the only way to remember them is through repetition and focus. You may also try saying things with different inflections or articulation. With a song it requires listening to it, singing it and playing it with and without your instrument. Tapping out rhythms which feel good may lead to some great phrases. Rhythmic feeling is vital to the language of music.

The twelve bar blues is probably the most commonly known song form to improvisers. It is therefore a perfect vehicle to experiment over. Perhaps a bit less common than Blues is the 32 bar, AABA form known to most jazzers as *Rhythm Changes* which is one of the most widely used song forms. Many blues style phrases also happen to fit nicely over Rhythm Changes. Here lies an opportunity to learn a great deal of music and improvisation while internalizing a song form which is used in hundreds if not thousands of tunes.

Grooves may change, harmonies may change, melodies may change in the playground set forth in this book and various, play-along CDs. *Bon Appétite!*

ACKNOWLEDGEMENTS

I wish to thank the following people:
Hans and Veronika Gruber for publishing this and so many beautiful works by other artists.

The musicians, Jerry Bergonzi, Ken Cervenka, Jeff Galindo, Russell Hoffman, Bob Kaufman and Matt Marvuglio for their beautiful musical contributions in the way of interpreting melodies and artistic improvisation.

DEDICATION

I would like to dedicate this project to the memory of Hans Gruber who has enriched the lives of so many people and contributed so much to musicians' growth and artistic development. Artists throughout the world have been inspired by his work and love for music. I am certain that this devotion which Hans and Veronika held for publishing beautiful books for musicians shall continue for many years to come.

Special thanks to Veronika Gruber for continuing the great work that comes from advance music.

Introduction

This is a play-along book of melodies and rhythm tracks which maintains a focus on one of the most common song forms (AABA) while exploring a wide range of rhythmic, melodic and harmonic variation. Its purpose is to demonstrate and provide a context in which melodic, improvisation can be experienced over tunes with comprehensive variations.

APPLICATIONS

1. Ear Training.
   Being that music is a sonic art form all systems of study are ultimately intended to get the player to be able to play what he or she hears and expand their ability to use the sonic language called music. In the end it's all about the ear. Learn these tunes by heart and you will expand your ear and musical vocabulary. After listening repeatedly try singing along and visualizing how the bass line and melody would play out on your instrument. Although techniques are demonstrated in the tunes, try simply hearing the melodies, bass lines, chord progressions and rhythm without having to label the specific devices, e.g.; scales, arpeggios, approaches, intervals, upper structure triads etc. Learn them by ear rather than always having to read the music although reading them is also great practice. Play by ear with all the tracks.

   Try playing back the same lines or new lines. Transcribe the bass parts and/or chord progressions from **CD1**, tracks **15, 16, 18, 21, 23, 24** and **30–34**.

2. Learn melodic, bass line concepts for the tunes including approach notes, passing tones, intervals, sequences, reharmonizations etc. on bass, keyboards, guitar, trombone and any other instrument. Think of this as a quarter note melody.

3. Improvise over the rhythm tracks or respond to the melodies with counter lines and rhythms.

4. Compose your own melodies over the rhythm tracks or write counter lines, harmony parts to play with the melodies. Compose bass lines and grooves. Experiment with the time. If you have recording equipment it is incredible practice to play and record all the parts.

5. Accompany the melodies and solos with chords, bass lines, rhythms and/or backgrounds.

6. Play by ear with all the tracks. Try playing back the same lines or new lines. Transcribe the lines and chord progressions.

7. Reharmonize over and over with the drums and bass line only. Discover new chord and voicing possibilities. Try superimposing other keys and using modal interchanges.

8. Play duets or trios by performing two or three melodies simultaneously. This will help you hear multiple lines and cross rhythms all at once.

9. Use the drum and bass only tracks to create the chords and melody. This is a great challenge in keeping the form without having the bass line or chords to keep you straight. It's all up to you!

10. Transpose the melodies over tracks in other keys.

11. Phrasing can develop as you articulate the melodies with different accents and inflections. Attack all notes or slur notes, try different ways of swinging the phrases and employing a triplet feel.

12. Reading and interpreting melodies, bass lines and chords.

Tunes are grouped in the following chapters according to the melodic/rhythmic concept.
- Diatonic melodies and approaches
- Rhythmic melodies, accents, groupings and riffs
- Pentatonic and blues scale melodies
- Diminished melodies and upper structure triads
- Intervalic melodies
- Combinations of the above.

HOW TO USE THE PLAY-ALONG

There are three CDs with this text. Bass is in the right channel, piano in the left and drums and horns are mostly in the center. Using the balance control of your stereo you may eliminate the bass or piano on all three discs.

Disc 1 (rhythm section only – melodic bass line examples)

With these tracks you may play the entire song including the bass line, melody and solo improvisation. Tracks **2** and **3** provide bass line approach examples. The tracks following are "2" feel, complete walking lines and other rhythmic styles which employ the approaches. Try the bass lines and melodies at different tempos, in alternate keys, or over pedal points and various grooves (swing, funk, hip hop, latin, jazz, waltz).

Tracks **4–18** and **30, 33, 34** are all in the concert key of B♭. This provides a range of possibilities in terms of rhythm section tracks over which you can play the bass lines, melodies and improvise.

Tracks **10–18** are slight reharmonizations yet the key remains B♭. Other tracks have bass lines in other keys. You may also transpose the B♭ bass lines and melodies then play them over the following keys:

Key of C, tracks **17** &**18** (medium swing)
Key of F, tracks **19**, (Bossa) **20**, (up swing) **21** (6/4 jazz waltz) and **29** (pedal point)
Key of E♭, track **22** (Mambo)
Key of A♭, track **23** (fast swing)
Key of D♭, track **24** (medium swing)
Key of G, track **25** (medium up swing) and **30** (medium up swing)
Key of A, track **26** (medium swing)
Key of D, track **27** (medium swing)

Disc 2

Disc 2 supplies the melodies without the solos over the same rhythm tracks. Here you can practice playing along with the recorded melody and then play your own improvised solo. Some tracks are short (2 choruses) which can help discipline you to play a concise statement. Other tracks are longer providing more room to stretch out.

Disc 3

Disc 3 can function as a complete demo or album to hear all the parts working together. Each tune is complete with rhythm, melody and solos. You can transcribe (write down) the solos for an excellent educational experience or just try figuring out the melodic lines and phrasing while playing along. Playing along with recordings is one of the most common ways to get it together. This play-along series provides the complete tracks on disc 3 and the minus one tracks on discs 1 and 2. Repeated listening will help get the music seated in your ear. If you are a rhythm player such as guitarist, pianist, bassist or drummer using discs 2 & 3 will enable you to practice accompanying the melodies and solos. Disc 3 is also a nice recording for general listening pleasure.

BUILDING A JAZZ VOCABULARY

Building a jazz vocabulary is much like learning to speak a language. Once you've internalized and mastered words and phrases you have a vocabulary. Your style of speaking evolves from manipulating the vocabulary to express different thoughts and feelings. Internalizing melodies, chord changes and rhythm will be our vocabulary. At the same time we listen to ourselves and others speak or play (music) which influences our use of vocabulary in the way of responses to what we hear.

In music we take the phrases and put them over different rhythms and harmonies framing the same notes in different pictures or sound environments. The melodies, rhythms and harmonies in this book can be used and interchanged over many sonic landscapes. As you practice the tunes internalize as much as possible and try to place the new vocabulary over different musical terrain by interchanging parts or all phrases over the variations and reharmonizations. Move ideas over by one or more eighth notes or several beats. Change the rhythm by using more or less notes and adding or subtracting triplets. Any and all ways of manipulating this vocabulary will help you gain strong listening skills and the ability to be more spontaneous in musical situations.

Part of the benefit of working with variations on the same piece is a perfect microcosm of the idea stated above and should help with the internalization process.

RHYTHM CHANGES

Rhythm changes have definite ties to the blues and are almost as old. Used as a musical vehicle for endless improvisations and melodies this form and progression have been and continue to be the impetus for hundreds of tunes.

As an educational tool rhythm changes provide a perfect balance of form and harmonic structure on which to practice thousands of ideas. This book will open some doors into the huge multitude of possibilities through the exposition of a wide variety of techniques demonstrated over the tune. Also a number of variations to the harmonic rhythm and reharmonizations are given in the way of pedal points and/or alternate chord changes. As with all improvisation the possibilities seem endless. By focussing on the same basic form over time one can experience a sense of familiarity and comfort while trying new ideas.

Each chapter has examples of rhythmic, melodic and harmonic techniques in the form of heads (melodies) composed over the tune. There is no necessary, consecutive order to the chapters and one may open the book and begin anywhere. The bass line chapter is useful for bass, trombone, keyboards, guitar, voice, saxophone, composition and anyone who wishes to expand their bass line concept or quarter note, melody.

The play-along CDs are useful for hearing many ideas over the chord changes. Play with melodic backgrounds, create your own harmony/counter parts, interchange melodies, compose your own riffs/melodies, compose your own harmony, play trio with bass and drums or piano and drums. Play quartet by adding your instrument to the trio (sax, bass and drums, piano, bass and drums or sax, drums and piano). Try free style, blues, pentatonic, intervalic, bebop and other approaches. Practice accents and rhythmic ideas. Try writing a rhythm and then put notes to it over the tune. Use the simple rhythmic melodies for backgrounds to solo with. You can get as creative as you like in the ways to use these materials.

SELF STUDY

1. Rhythm and time feel

Try singing and tapping in time by repeating a figure against a consistent pulse such as 4/4. You can do the same in 3/4. Eventually you may put the 3 against the 4 or vice versa by singing and tapping them simultaneously. Accent different beats that feel natural. Some accents may not feel natural at first, however, as you get used to the sound they will feel more natural.

Hooking up with other players rhythmically requires good listening skills and a familiar vocabulary of accents and polyrhythms. Listening to and transcribing recordings is an excellent way to broaden your rhythmic vocabulary. Sing and tap as you listen. Play along on your instrument

2. Tonal and non-tonal harmony

If you try every major pentatonic scale over the same bass note and examine the tones above (i.e. 5, 7, 1, #9, 11 or b5, b6, b7, b9, #9) you would discover all the possibilities. Then try every minor pentatonic over the same bass note. Listen and decide which of them sound good and which do not work. Write down what you learn. You may do the same exercise with all triads, scales, modes and melodic ideas. In addition try playing all keys and ideas over the same chord. Write down what you learn and try using the ideas over changes.

THE A A B A FORM

Rhythm Changes provide a perfect example of a standard, 32 bar, song form. It is easily divided into four 8 bar sections or phrases, **A A B A** with the **A** sections all resembling the first 8 bars and the **B** section being a definite contrast, both rhythmically (different harmonic rhythm) and harmonically (different chord progression). This gives the improvising musician or student a great vehicle to study form and melodic development. For the bassist it is an opportunity to work out lines over two or up to eight beats per chord.

Seeing the form blocked out in the following two examples helps create a mental picture of the song form.

Visualizing and hearing the big picture (whole song) while playing each beat will help your phrasing and prevent you from getting lost.

Example 1

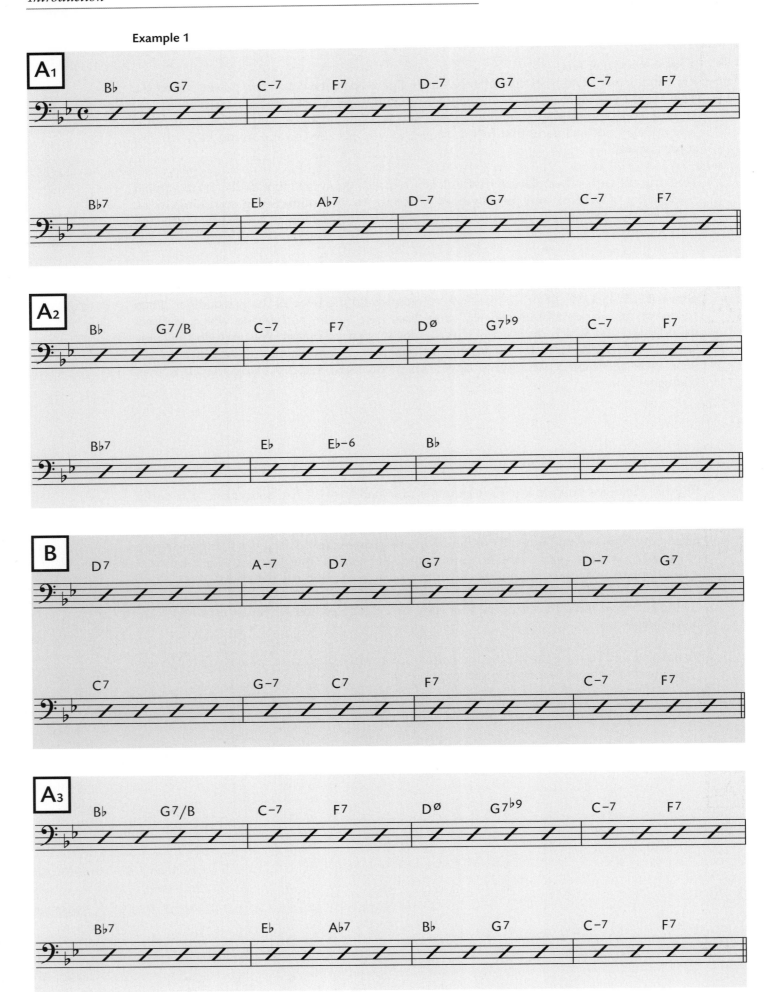

Example 2

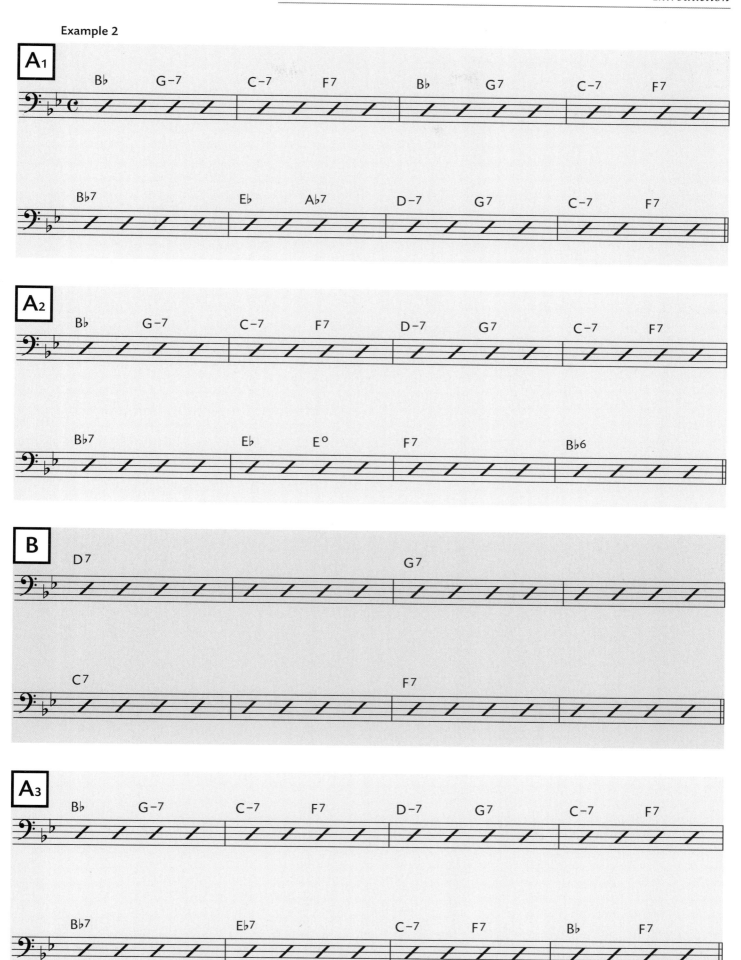

Part I

BASS LINES

The short bass line examples, 1–10 (p. 24f.), demonstrate various approaches and melodic techniques. Practice them repeatedly and then try your own versions.

A basic "2" feel is an emphasis on beats one and three with two half notes in a measure or two quarter notes on one and three and rests on beats two and four. When embellishing a "2" feel, occasional walking or fills can be added, leading into a chord change or the next phrase. These fills will almost always lead to a down beat resulting in the most comfortable phrasing. It will be obvious when fills do not feel natural. The time should flow naturally with the phrases of the chord progression.

In jazz music this chord progression *(rhythm changes)* became popular in the swing and bebop eras as it provides a good vehicle for improvisation with its diatonic **A** section and its semi modal **B** section or bridge. Pay attention to the diatonic sequences and intervals employed in the lines along with various approach notes, passing tones and alternate scales such as diminished, pentatonic, whole tone and Lydian♭7.

Listening is a great way, if not the best, to learn music. Transcribing (writing down) what you hear will help to strengthen your musical ear, sense of phrasing, rhythm and dynamics. You are encouraged to use the CDs for transcriptions. There are some blank pages to get you started.

The accompanying CDs have versions at different tempos for practicing. Play along with or without the bass (in the right channel only) when reading the written lines and then practice walking your own lines over the rhythm tracks minus the bass. It is also very helpful to write your own bass lines. Think quarter note, melody.

But first, on the following four pages, I will give you some hints on how to develop your own ideas starting from simple bass lines with roots and chord notes only then gradually employing more melodic lines with chromatic passing tones and implied dominants.

REHARMONIZATIONS

There are a lot of reharmonizations for Rhythm Changes out in the wild. I have included some examples to give you a general idea about what is possible in terms of secondary dominants, substitutions and even Coltrane-like progressions where new tonal centers are introduced temporarily – usually in intervals of major thirds. Slash chords indicate an intended upper structure such as a triad or seventh chord over an alternate bass note or other chord. If the lower letter is not followed by a suffix (E/G) it means the bottom is just a bass note but if the symbol reads E/G7 it means an E major triad over a G7 chord.

TRANSPOSITIONS

Of course, Rhythm Changes are not confined to the key of B♭ and you should be able to play them in all twelve keys. To emphasize this point, **CD1** includes some of the lines in different but common keys. Some of these lines are not literal transpositions but feature a few alterations.

WHERE THE PASSING TONES COME FROM

Every chord has one or more scales which contain the chord tones (1, 3, 5, 7) and a set of passing tones (2, 4, 6). Diatonic, scale, passing tones come from the chord scale. They can be whole steps or half steps depending on the scale. Chromatic passing tones are always half steps. Below in the B♭ scales, chord tones are marked with an arrow and all other notes are passing tones.

B♭ Major scale (diatonic)

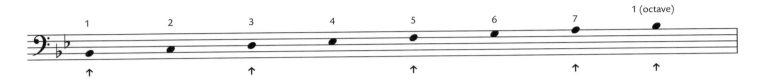

B♭ Chromatic scale (half-tones)

Below are some I VI II V harmonic phrases where the bass line employs scale and chromatic passing tones. Numbers indicate relationships to the chord on which the notes occur.

Observe that the VI (G7) chord is dominant here. This is common where the VI7 functions as V7 of II (C–7). This is known as a *secondary dominant*. Other I VI II V progressions may use VI–7.

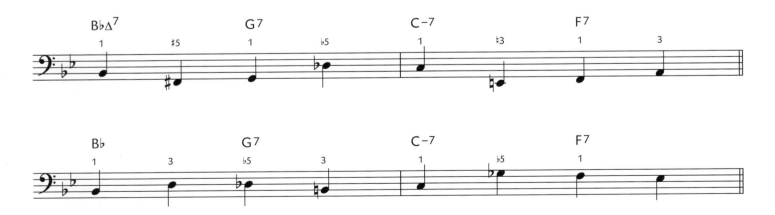

QUICK REFERENCE FOR CHORD TONES & PASSING TONES

Chord Type	Chord Tones	Passing Tones (Scale)
Δ7	1, 3, 5, 7	2, 4, 6
Δ7♭5	1, 3, ♭5, 7	2, 4, 6
Δ7♯5	1, 3, ♯5, 7	2, ♯4, 6
−7	1, ♭3, 5, ♭7	2, 4, 6
°7	1, ♭3, ♭5, ♭♭7	2, 4, ♭6, 7
∅7 (−7♭5)	1, ♭3, ♭5, ♭7	♭2, 4, ♭6
∅♮9	1, ♭3, ♭5, ♭7	2, 4, ♭6
Δ6	1, 3, 5, 6	2, 4, 7
−6	1, ♭3, 5, 6	2, 4, 7
−Δ7	1, ♭3, 5, 7	2, 4, 6
Dominant 7	1, 3, 5, ♭7	2, 4, 6
Dom. 7 ♯11	1, 3, 5, ♭7	2, ♯4, 6
Dom. 7 ♯5 (augmented)	1, 3, ♯5, ♭7	2, ♯4
Dom. 7sus4	1, 4, 5, ♭7	2, 3, 6
Dom. 7 ♭9	1, 3, 5, ♭7	♭2, ♯2, 4, 6
Dom. 7 ♭9 ♮13	1, 3, 5, ♭7	♭2, ♯2, ♯4, 6
Dom. 7 altered	1, 3, ♭5, ♭7	♭2, ♯2, ♭6
Dom. 7 ♭5	1, 3, ♭5, ♭7	2, 4, 6

This list shows scale passing tones only. Many more variations exist with chromatic passing tones or approaches, particularly with the dominant chords.

Disc **1**
Track 2 (slow)
Track 3 (medium)

VARIATIONS OF MELODIC BASS LINES
ON THE FIRST FOUR MEASURES OF RHYTHM CHANGES

Example 1a | *Roots only*

Example 1b | *Roots and fifths*

Example 2 | *Roots, thirds, fifths and sevenths with scale and chromatic passing tones*

Example 3 | *Diatonic triad and seventh arpeggios resulting in occasional inversions on chord beats*

Example 4 | *Melodic scale sequences*

Example 5 | *Melodic scale sequences with chromaticism and implied secondary dominant (A7)*

Example 6 | *Melodic sequences yielding scale passages across barlines and occasional non-chord tones on chord beats*

Example 7a & b | *Scale and chromatic lines which result in working substitute bass notes on chord-beats (bebop scale)*

Example 8 | *Diatonic triads with chromatic approach*

Example 9 | *Chromaticism and scale approach*

Example 10 | *Major and minor sixth intervals*

LINE 1A

Disc **1**
Track 4
(1st chorus)

A 2-feel bass line. Here the emphasis lies on beats one and three.

LINE 1B

Disc **1**
Track 4
(2nd chorus)

Basic roots and fifths provide solid chord outline.

Disc **1**
Track 4

Transcribe bass line 3rd chorus

LINE 1C

Disc **1**
Track 5
(1st chorus)

Roots, thirds and fifths along with scale and chromatic approaches leading into roots provide solid chord outlines with interesting melodic shapes and directions.

Transcribe bass line 2nd chorus

LINE 2

Roots, thirds, fifths and sevenths along with scale and chromatic approaches. Here an occasional inversion (3rd, 5th or 7th) takes the place of the root on a chord-beat.

Disc **1**
Track 6
(1st chorus)

LINE 3

Disc **1**
Track 7
(1st chorus)

LINE 4

Disc **1**
Track 7
(2nd chorus)

LINE 5

Disc **1**
Track 7
(3rd chorus)

(End)

LINE 6

Disc **1**
Track 8
(1st chorus)

There is a strong emphasis on chromatic approach, sequenced motives, scale-wise movement and arpeggios of chord inversions in the lines on track 8 (#6, #7 and #8).

LINE 7

Disc **1**
Track 8
(2nd chorus)

LINE 8

Disc 1
Track 8
(3rd chorus)

LINE 9

Disc **1**
Track 9
(1st chorus)

The lines on Track 9 (#9, #10, #11) go even further in exploring the principles introduced on track 8. These very melodic lines emphasize the high register of the bass.

LINE 10

Disc **1**
Track 9
(2nd chorus)

LINE 11

Disc **1**
Track 9
(3rd chorus)

REHARMONIZATION 1

Tritone subtitution (e.g. D♭7 for G7, watch for more) leads to smooth chromatic movement in the bass line. Transcribe the 2nd and 3rd choruses of this and the following tracks.

Disc 1
Track 10

REHARMONIZATION 2

Disc **1**
Track 11

Measures 1 and 2 of the **A** sections feature a flamenco-like root movement, while the **B** section uses tritone substitution for a strictly chromatic harmonic movement.

Transcribe the 2nd and 3rd choruses.

REHARMONIZATION 3

Disc **1**
Track 12

Only the first two **A** sections are reharmonized. The tonal center shifts to G♭ and D occasionally and there are plenty of secondary dominants and tritone substitutions.

Transcribe the 2nd and 3rd choruses.

REHARMONIZATION 4

This example features "slash chords" in the **A** sections with upper structure chords in chromatic movement. Also, the tonal center changes to G♭ and D occasionally.

Transcribe the 2nd and 3rd choruses.

REHARMONIZATION 5

This reharmonization combines some of the afore-mentioned techniques.

Disc **1**
Track 14

Transcribe the 2nd and 3rd choruses.

REHARMONIZATION 6

Disc **1**
Track 15

A sections: half time swing/funk over B♭7
B section: walk. The first four bars feature an alternate progression with II V of IV

simile

Transcribe the 2ⁿᵈ and 3ʳᵈ choruses.

REHARMONIZATION 7

Disc **1**
Track 16

A section harmony is played over an F pedal, with a broken rhythmic feel. **B** sections are straightforward walking bass lines. Transcribe all three choruses.

REHARMONIZATION 8

Disc **1**
Track 17

Here the bridge (section **B**) is completely reinterpreted with E♭ – the IV of B♭ – as new tonal center (mind the key signature).

Transcribe the 2nd chorus.

REHARMONIZATION 9

The use of diminished and half-diminished chords and ♭9s in the dominant chords gives this reharmonization a nice minor-like feeling. Also, note the substitutions in the **B** section.

Disc **1**
Track 18

Transcribe the 2ⁿᵈ chorus, too.

LINE 3 (C)

Disc 1
Track 19

You are already familiar with this bass line. Play it in the key of C this time.

Transcribe the 2nd chorus.

REHARMONIZATION 1 (C)

Disc **1**
Track 20

Another familiar line in the key of C.

Transcribe the 2nd chorus.

Disc **1**
Track 21

REHARMONIZATION 10

Try this Bossa in the key of F. Note the A–7 (III–7) as a substitute for the F major
on the first chord.

Transcribe the 2nd chorus.

LINE 9 (F)

Disc **1**
Track 22
(1st chorus)

Transcribe the 2nd chorus.

LINE 11A (F)

Disc 1
Track 22
(3rd chorus)

The range of the bass being limited, transposing line 11 one fifth down required octave shifts and alterations in some places. Compare this line to the original!

RHYTHM CHANGES IN 6/4

This example is in 6/4 time and in the key of F. Transcribe the bass part (the first 6 bars are given to get you started).

Disc **1**
Track 23

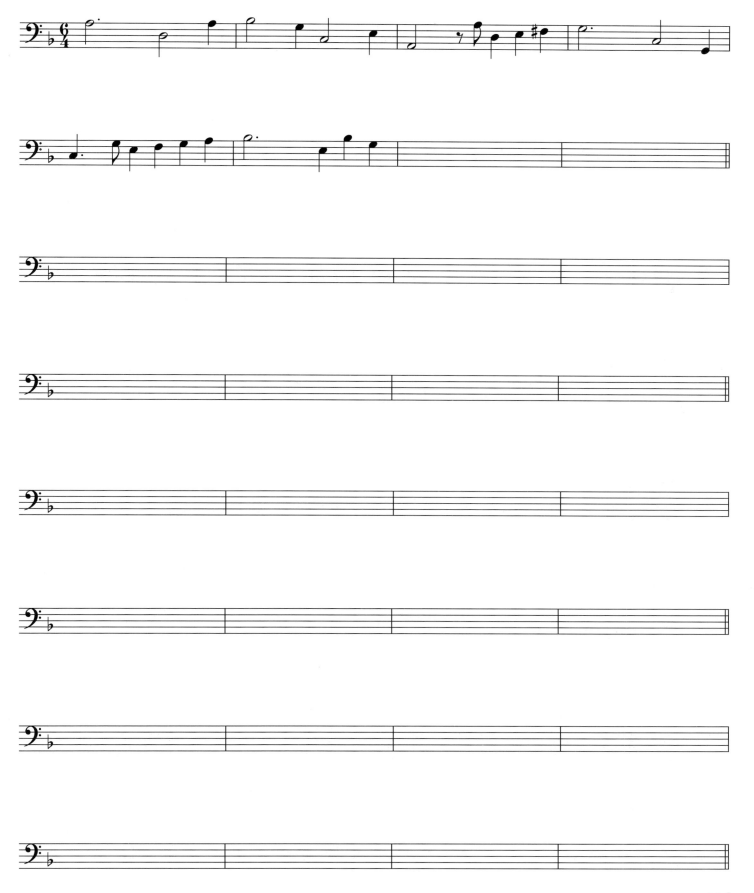

Eb MAMBO

Transcribe the bass part (2 choruses). The key is Eb.

LINE 1C (A♭)

Disc **1**
Track 25
(1st chorus)

Again, this line is not transposed literally but moved to a higher register, also. Compare this example to the original to find out which other alterations were made.

Transcribe the 2nd chorus.

LINE 11A (A♭)

Disc **1**
Track 25
(3rd chorus)

LINE 4 (D♭)

Disc **1**
Track 26

Transcribe the 2nd chorus.

LINE 9 (G)

Disc **1**
Track 27
(1st chorus)

LINE 11A (G)

Disc **1**
Track 27
(2nd chorus)

Transcribe the 3rd chorus.

LINE 4 (A)

Disc **1**
Track 28
(1st chorus)

LINE 12 (A)

This line makes use of symmetric diminished scales as introduced in bars 1–2 and 5–6 (see the difference?). Note the reharmonizations and the use of symmetrical intervalic motives.

Disc 1
Track 28
(2nd chorus)

LINE 13 (D)

Disc **1**
Track 29
(1st chorus)

This key, of course, allows for efficient use of open E, A and D strings which is applied here to provide a contrast between solid roots and high register "comments".

LINE 14 (D)

Disc **1**
Track 29
(2nd chorus)

Line #14 is constructed around pentatonic scales only.

OPEN CHANGES 1 (B♭)

Disc **1**
Track 30

Transcribe the bass line (6 choruses total).

OPEN CHANGES 2 (F)

Transcribe the bass part (4 choruses total).

Disc 1
Track 31

VARIATION 1 (G)

Disc 1
Track 32

Transcribe the bass part (4 choruses total).

FREE STYLE 1

This is the line behind "The Lizard of Odds" (slow version) on page 142 (disc 2, track 21). Note the 8 bar intro. Complete the transcription.

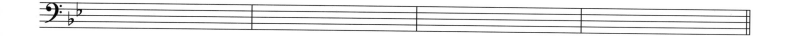

FREE STYLE 2

This is the line behind the fast version of "The Lizard of Odds" on page 142 (disc 2, track 22). Complete the transcription.

SUGGESTED LISTENING

BASSISTS

Pops Foster, Walter Page, Curley Russell, Israel Crosby, Tommy Potter, Jimmy Blanton, Milt Hinton, George Duvivier, Wendel Marshall, Monk Montgomery, Wilbur Ware, Oscar Pettiford, Charles Mingus, Aaron Bell, Sam Jones, Ray Brown, Leroy Vinnegar, Percy Heath, Slam Stewart, Lonnie Plaxico, Larry Grenadier, Red Mitchell, Richard Davis, Walter Booker, Bob Cranshaw, Doug Watkins, Jimmy Garrison, Art Davis, Paul Chambers, James Jamerson, Gary Peacock, Scott LaFaro, Chuck Israels, Charlie Haden, Ron Carter, Reggie Workman, Arvell Shaw, Jimmy Merit, Steve Davis, Earl May, Butch Warren, Teddy Kotick, Tommy Williams, George Mraz, Eddie Gomez, Dave Holland, Miroslav Vitous, Herbie Lewis, Steve Swallow, Ray Drummond, Rodney Whitaker, Niels-Henning Ørsted Pedersen, Jay Leonhart, Carol Kaye, Michael Moore, Rufus Reid, Palle Danielson, Peter Washington, Stanley Clarke, Mike Richmond, Scott Lee, Gene Perla, Dennis Irwin, Jaco Pastorius, Scott Colly, Marc Johnson, Robert Hurst, Charles Fambrough, John Clayton, John Patitucci, James Genus, Ben Wolf, Harvie S, Lynn Seaton, Kristin Korb, Avishai Cohen, Christian McBride, and many others.

BOP & POST-BOP LEADERS

Charlie Parker, Dizzy Gillespie, Woody Herman, Duke Ellington, Bud Powell, Thelonious Monk, Wynton Kelly, Wes Montgomery, Miles Davis, John Coltrane, Sonny Rollins, Clifford Brown, Lee Konitz, Cannonball Adderley, Jackie Byard, Mal Waldron, Red Garland, J.J. Johnson, Oscar Peterson, Curtis Fuller, Kenny Dorham, Freddie Hubbard, Cedar Walton, Donald Byrd, Zoot Sims, Al Cohn, Wayne Shorter, Jackie McClean, Horace Silver, Lee Morgan, Ahmad Jamal, Dexter Gordon, Ben Webster, Eddie Harris, James Moody, Al Haig, Sonny Clark, Charles Mingus, Nat Adderley, Hank Jones, Eric Dolphy, Milt Jackson, John Lewis, McCoy Tyner, Bill Evans, Woody Shaw, Joe Henderson, Hank Mobley, Gene Emmans, Herbie Hancock, Chick Corea, Keith Jarrett, Victor Feldman, Bobby Hutcherson, Charles Lloyd, Gary Burton, Chet Baker, Joe Farrell, Stan Getz, Hampton Hawes, Art Blakey, Max Roach, Tony Williams, Ornette Coleman, Don Cherry, Dewey Redman, Yusef Lateef, Michael and Randy Brecker, Elvin Jones, Roy Haynes, Dave Liebman, Herbie Nichols, Steve Grossman, John McLaughlin, Jerry Bergonzi, Bob Berg, Tom Harrell, Bob Brookmeyer, Steve Lacey, Sam Rivers, Anthony Braxton, Hal Crook, Albert Ayler, Lester Bowie, Albert Mangelsdorff and many more.

Many of the bassists listed above are also leaders of groups.

Me and my daughter Eva
(Photo: Nicole Goodhue)

Part 2
Play-Along

DIATONIC MELODIES

Diatonic refers to tones of the major and minor scales. The diatonic melodies in the following chapter employ upper and lower auxiliary tones as well as approach notes and melodic sequences. In some cases the bridge, melody uses other scales such as symmetric, diminished, whole tone or Lydian ♭7. In modern times diatonic can also mean related to modes and other scales which is fairly broad.

The first group of melodies in this book are for the most part diatonic to the key with exception to chromatic approach notes and various tensions used over the dominant chords of the **B** section (bridge), to provide contrast.

Scales can be the source of almost any melodic material as they contain arpeggios, intervals and can be sequenced and chromaticised. In addition to learning the melodies in the book/CD work on creating melodies from the tones of a scale. Experiment with rhythms and intervals.

Hop on the Scale, Peaceful Resolution and *Snake Shoes* are fully diatonic to the key with the use of chromatic approach above and/or below chord tones. Over the **B** sections the same tunes have diatonic melodies relative to the chord scales. Often in jazz, improvisers will substitute scales to provide a new color or tension. Practicing diatonic melodies is a necessary step toward developing your ear and jazz vocabulary.

DIATONIC SCALES AND MODES

Most students will already be familiar with modes derived from the major and the various minor scales, the related chords and arpeggios. But how to put this knowledge into effective use when constructing a melody often seems to be the more difficult part. Especially the minor scales and modes offer surprising possibilities that are often overlooked.

Also, the difference between modes and harmonic function can be confusing. Very simply put, in a functional context dominant chords create a tension that needs to be resolved, if only temporarily – e.g. G7 → CΔ or A7 → D7 → G7 → CΔ. The chords "lead" somewhere (dominant) or rest on a tonic. There are, of course, a lot of techniques to deceive the ear and create surprising resolutions some of which were used for the reharmonizations in Part I. In analysis these interrelations of chords within a given tonality are usually denoted with roman numerals plus options – e.g. V7 → IΔ7.

In a strict modal context, there is no such thing as "V7 → I". It is rather the "color" of the chords and associated scales that create the texture of a piece and a chord symbol like "FΔ7♯11" would not denote the subdominant of C major (IV) but simply F Lydian mode as both scale and chord.

Music would be very boring if rules and concepts were only applied strictly and to the letter. In contemporary jazz modal and functional approaches often are mixed and quite successfully so. The following pages are included to give you an idea about how to arrive at convincing melodies from diatonic scales and modes.

MODES AND DIATONIC CHORDS OF THE MAJOR SCALE

Example 1 | *Major scale and relative minor scale, possible seventh chords, functions and modes*

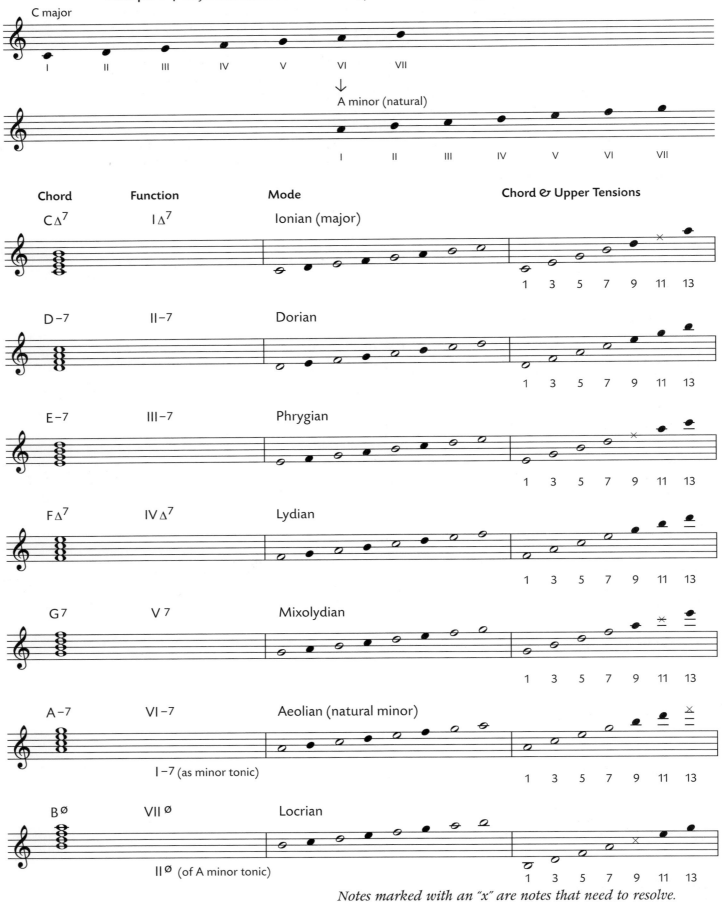

Chord   Function   Mode   Chord & Upper Tensions

Notes marked with an "x" are notes that need to resolve.

FORMS OF MINOR SCALES

Other than its relative major scale the natural (or pure) minor scale lacks a major seventh. That means, in a harmonic context you cannot build a dominant seventh chord on the V – the result is a minor seventh chord. So, early in the history of European music composers altered the minor scale and used a major seventh instead of a minor seventh. For obvious reasons this scale is called "harmonic minor" and the famous V7♭9 chord originally was derived from this scale. Since the resulting augmented second between the (minor) sixth and the major seventh was found aesthetically unpleasing, the sixth eventually was altered, too. This scale is known as "melodic minor".

In traditional European music the direction in which a melodic line evolved did matter: upward motion required melodic minor, downward motion natural minor. In modern jazz, however, this distinction is not made.

Example 1 | *Natural minor (also pure or relative minor), Aeolian mode*

Example 2 | *Harmonic minor*

Example 3 | *Traditional melodic minor (ascending and descending)*

Example 4 | *Real melodic minor (jazz minor)*

Example 5 | *Scale from 5ᵗʰ degree of A harmonic minor, also known as HM5 mode*

Example 6 | *Resolution of a V7♭9 chord to I–7 tonic*

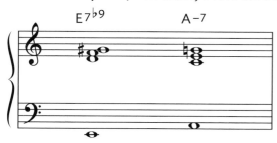

MODES, CHORDS AND TENSIONS OF THE HARMONIC MINOR SCALE

Try substituting the minor modes for the major modes, for example, use Dorian♯11 in place of Dorian. Experiment!

MODES, CHORDS AND TENSIONS OF THE JAZZ (MELODIC) MINOR SCALE

APPROACH NOTES

Basic Arpeggios

Example 1 | *Single chromatic approach from below*

Example 2 | *Single chromatic approach from above*

Example 3 | *Double chromatic approach from below*

Example 4 | *Double chromatic approach from above*

Example 5 | *Single scale approach from above*

Example 6 | *Single scale approach from below*

Example 7 | *Double scale approach from above*

C−7 (Dorian) approaching all chord tones   C−7 approaching 3rd only

Example 8 | *Double scale approach from below*

C−7 (Dorian) approaching all chord tones   C−7 approaching root & 5th

DIATONIC TRIADS

Example 1 | *Major scale triads*

Example 2 | *Inversions of triads*

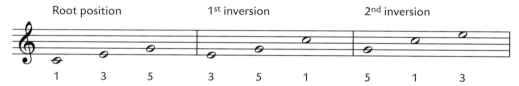

Example 3 | *Permutations of triads*

As upper structures – diatonic or non-diatonic – all 5 types of triads (major, minor, augmented, diminished and sus4), may also be permutated.

Example 4 | *Permutations in a melodic context*

Note: approaches may be applied to triads (see *I'm Thinking* and *Chin Up*)

TRIADS FROM CHORD SCALES

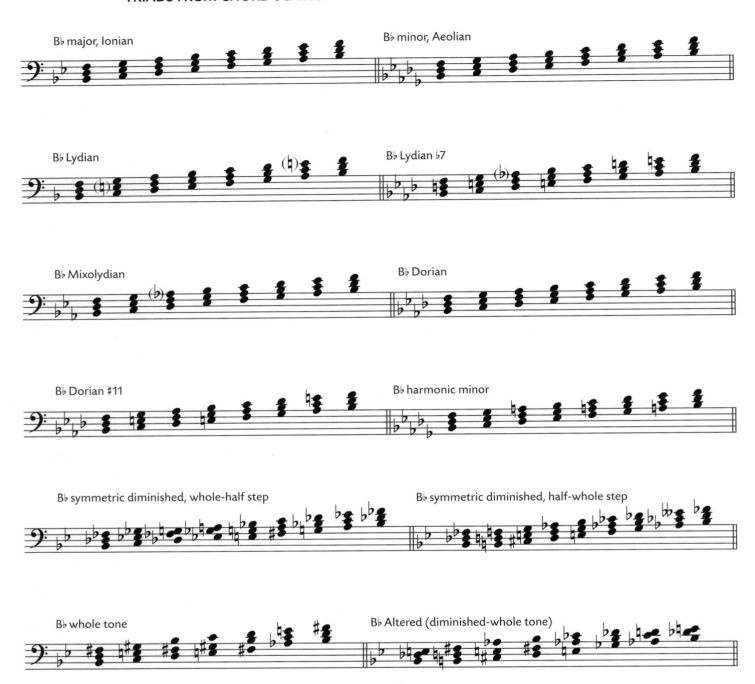

RANDOM DIATONIC INTERVALS

One complete chorus as a study in random diatonic intervals.

HOP ON THE SCALE

Bruce Gertz

HOP ON THE SCALE

C concert

Bruce Gertz

PEACEFUL RESOLUTION

Bruce Gertz

(Turnaround)

PEACEFUL RESOLUTION

Disc 2
Track 4
or
Disc 1
Track 24

CHIN UP
Mambo

Bruce Gertz

bass

CHIN UP
Mambo

C concert

Bruce Gertz

RED STAR

Bruce Gertz

Disc **2**
Track 5

bass

RED STAR

C concert

Bruce Gertz

SNAKE SHOES

Bruce Gertz

SNAKE SHOES

C concert

Bruce Gertz

BROILED

Disc **2**
Track 7

Bruce Gertz

BROILED

C concert

Bruce Gertz

RHYTHMIC MELODIES

Melodies are given life when put to rhythm. The feeling of time when played strong is unmistakable and commands attention. Rhythm is up lifting and gives flight to music. There are infinite ways to treat a melody with rhythm.

Accents

The best place to start is with accents of only one note, perhaps a tonic or dominant (fifth), of the key. Then try other notes. You can make a strong statement with the use of accents. The following heads were built on accents: *The Rhythm Method, Kicks, Don't Pick It Up, Car Horn 1&2, Hit Me and Chin Up.* Some are simple one note melodies, however, the accents give them life. Although there may not be many notes here the rhythms can pose a challenge. These kinds of exercises will strengthen time and phrasing. After playing the melodies in the book try playing and writing your own accent melodies. Notice how a melody has a different meaning coming first from the rhythm rather than the notes.

Riffs

Riffs are repeated phrases (usually short) which fly over the changes with strong motivic ideas. Often blues scales or licks are used for melodies or background riffs. They contribute to the power of the groove with their rhythmic consistency. In some ways riffs are similar to *Montuno* parts in Latin music. Try using the riff melodies in the book as backgrounds, to a solo or one of the other melodies. Invent new riffs of your own and think rhythmically.

Groupings

When notes are grouped together in a consistent number or sequence of numbers it can be very effective. For example, the tunes *Hit Me* (3 note groupings in the **A** section, 4 note groupings in the **B** section), *Don't Pick It Up* (2 note ideas throughout), *Penta-Rhythm* (4 note groupings), *Riff Off* (4 note groupings, **A** section, 4 & 6 note groupings, **B** section). Look for groupings in other tunes.

Hemiola

When a consistent rhythm crosses the time like going against the grain it is known as hemiola. The tune *Don't Pick It Up* crosses the bar line with its rhythmic displacement of the same two note idea first beginning on beat one and then on the up beat of 3. *Penta-Rhythm* crosses the bar line with a 4 note melodic rhythm first from beat 1 and then from beat 4. Other tunes with hemiolas are *You First, Riff Off, Stress Test* and more.

Retrograde

When you reverse the rhythm of the line so as to write or play it backwards that is a retrograde of the rhythm. You may also retrograde the intervals to get a mirror image of the line. The bridge of *Red Note Special* begins with a retrograde rhythm of the **A** section.

Contrast

It is most effective to use rhythmic contrast between phrases or sections of the tune. An example would be the use of consistent eighth notes on a section and then half notes, whole notes or rests in another section. *Horse Power, Rhythm a Dim, Penta-Rhythm, The Lizard of Odds, Quarts & Fifths, Ring Around Uranus* and other tunes express rhythmic contrast between the **A** section and bridge as well as space in the melody.

Polyrhythm:

Different time signatures can be played in the same space like the gears in a clock or the planetary orbits. When we play three beats in the space of two (quarter note, triplets), it is called a polyrhythm. Other polyrhythms might be 5 over 4, 5 over 3, 7 over 4, 9 over 4 etc. *Ring Around Uranus* has quarter note triplets throughout the bridge implying a metric modulation from 4/4 to 6/4 time.

THE RHYTHM METHOD

Bruce Gertz

Disc **2**
Track 8
or
Disc 1
Track 25

THE RHYTHM METHOD

C concert

Bruce Gertz

KICKS

Bruce Gertz

Disc **2**
Track 9

KICKS

C concert

Bruce Gertz

CAR HORNS

(1st part)

In this chordless trio setting the changes are interpreted freely, yet the form is adhered to.

Bruce Gertz

Disc 2
Track 10
or
Disc 1
Tracks 8 (slow)
& 30

bass

CAR HORNS
(2nd Part)

bass

Bruce Gertz

(end on Bb7/E)

CAR HORNS
(1st part)

Bruce Gertz

CAR HORNS
(2nd Part)

C concert

Bruce Gertz

HIT ME

Disc **2**
Track 11

Bruce Gertz

2 choruses, end on F∆7

HIT ME

C concert

Bruce Gertz

2 choruses, end on $F\Delta^7$

DON'T PICK IT UP

Bruce Gertz

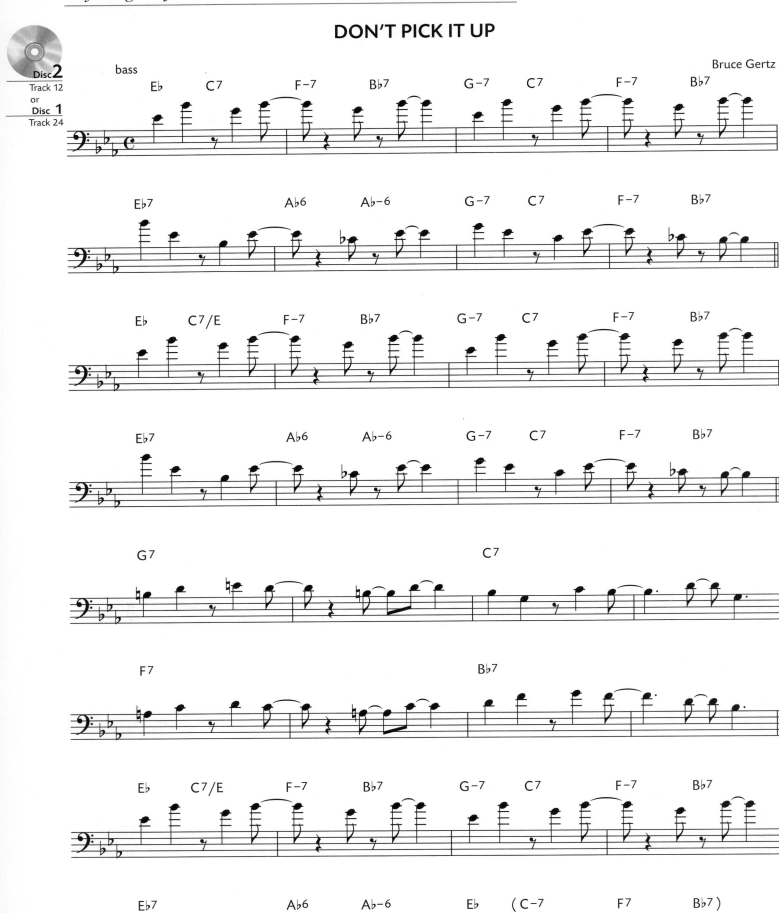

DON'T PICK IT UP

C concert

Bruce Gertz

PENTATONIC AND
BLUES SCALE MELODIES

There are many possibilities for five note scales *(pentatonic)*. The scales shown are basic major and minor versions followed by modest, chromatic alterations. Many blues scales are variations of these pentatonic scales. The intervalic structure of these scales can make for angular melodies while the use of chromaticism can temper the angles. The presence of perfect fourths and fifths as well as sus4 triads is characteristic to the pentatonics. *Penta-Rhythm, Riff Off, Overweight and Underpaid, Pentup Bop, Penta Roll, Not Yet, The Lizard of Odds* are all examples of pentatonic melodies. Many of the remaining melodies in the book also contain some pentatonics.

Notice how major and minor pentatonic melodies both sound good but different over the chords. On the bridges of *Penta-Rhythm* and *Riff Off* some different pentatonic tonalities are superimposed over the chords. On the **A** section of *The Lizard of Odds* chromaticism creates a bluesy, snake-in-the-grass quality.

Observe the rhythmic groupings and phrasing employed in the pentatonic melodies.

While reading and practicing the basic pentatonic scales, play them from each degree, one octave up and down to hear their modes.

Check to see the triads – major, minor, sus4, diminished – as well as the seventh or sixth chords you can find and use in each scale.

Break them up by skipping notes and explore the intervalic possibilities. Adding chromaticism can produce many variations including blues scales.

BASIC PENTATONIC SCALES

* *Kumoi* and *Hira* are traditional japanese scales (or, more precisely, tunings).

PENTATONIC SCALES OVER CHORDS

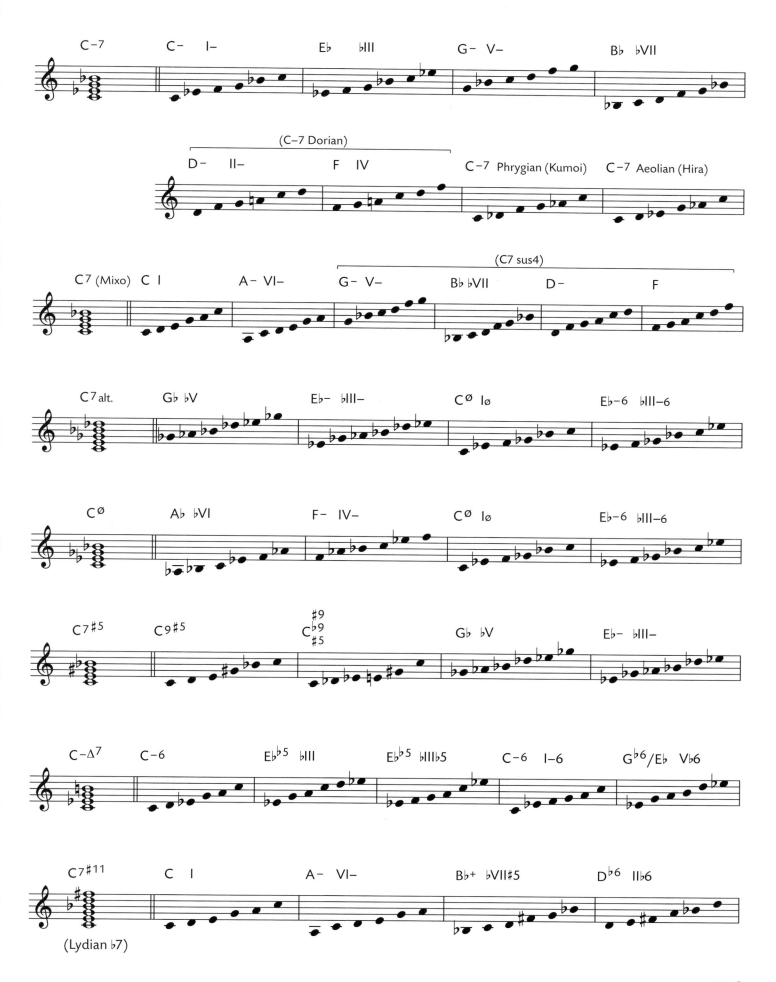

(Lydian ♭7)

PENTATONIC EXERCISES

Play these exercises in all keys. Play them retrograde (backwards). Try starting every next note in the sequence. Try different rhythms such as triplets, groupings or syncopations.

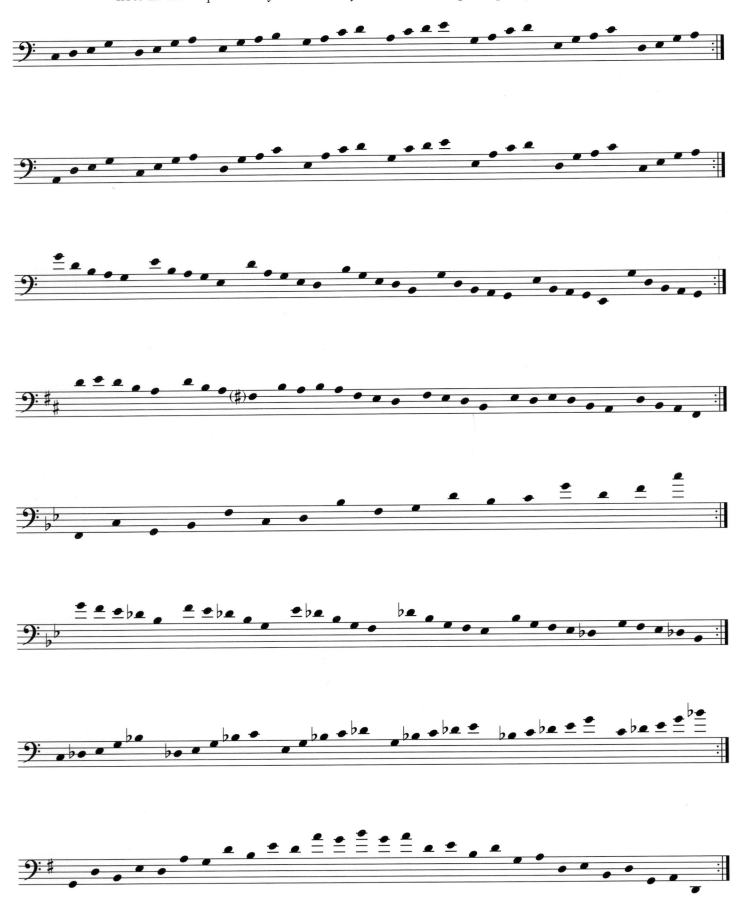

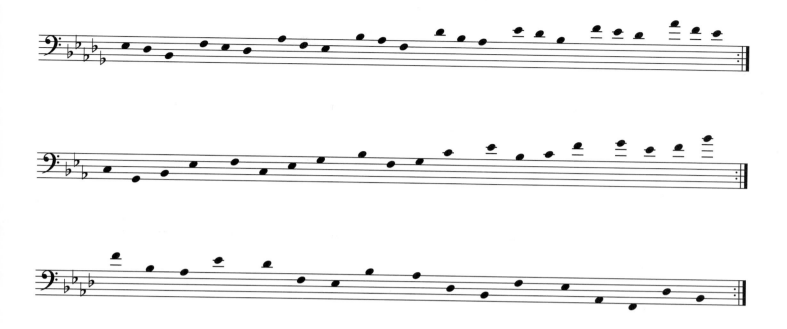

Melodic Study Over B Section Changes

Blues scales work well as both forms of minor and major pentatonic variations

PENTA-RHYTHM

All the **A** sections are B♭7 Funk/Hip Hop (half-time feel).
The **B** section is swing with chord changes.

Bruce Gertz

Disc 2
Track 13
or
Disc 1
Track 15

bass

PENTA-RHYTHM

All the **A** sections are B♭7 Funk/Hip Hop.
The **B** section is swing with chord changes.

Bruce Gertz

PENTUP BOP

Bruce Gertz

Disc **2**
Track 14

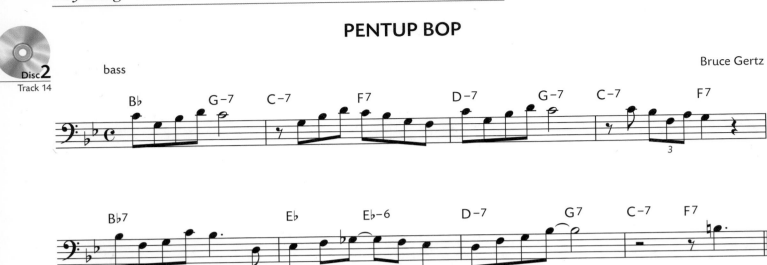

PENTUP BOP

C concert

Bruce Gertz

YOU FIRST

Bruce Gertz

YOU FIRST

C concert

Bruce Gertz

NOT YET

Bruce Gertz

bass

NOT YET

C concert

Bruce Gertz

RIFF OFF

All the **A** sections are B♭7 Funk/Hip Hop.
The **B** section is swing with chord changes.

Bruce Gertz

Disc 2
Track 17
or
Disc 1
Track 15

bass

RIFF OFF

All the **A** sections are Bb7 Funk/Hip Hop.
The **B** section is swing with chord changes.

Bruce Gertz

PENTA ROLL

Bruce Gertz

PENTA ROLL

C concert

Bruce Gertz

OVERWEIGHT AND UNDERPAID

Bruce Gertz

Disc **2**
Track 19
or
Disc **1**
Track 17

OVERWEIGHT AND UNDERPAID

C concert

Bruce Gertz

DIMINISHED MELODIES

Diminished scales yield seemingly infinite melodic possibilities and even more when combined with other scales. There are two forms of symmetric diminished scales with three transpositions each. First is the whole step/half step and second is the half step/whole step scale which is the same as starting on the second, fourth, sixth or eighth step of the first scale.

There are three types of triads, four types of seventh chords and two types of sixth chords all built on four tones, a minor third apart (root, ♭3, ♭5, ♭♭7) of the half step/whole step scale. Diminished triads and seventh chords are present at every step of the eight note scale. Although we think of flat fifth in diminished there are perfect fourths and fifths in the scale as well. Because it is a symmetrical scale all the same types of structures exist in minor third intervals. Look at a C7, half step/whole step scale and you will find C, E♭, G♭ and A triads, major, minor and diminished as well as dominant 7, minor 7, diminished 7, half-diminished 7, major 6 and minor 6 all built on the same four roots, a minor third apart. When you start combining these chords and mixing them with intervals and scale passages the possibilities seem endless.

Stress Test is 100% diminished. The **A** section is a scale melody and the **B** section uses a combination of scale passages and triads from the half/whole step scales of the dominant chords. Other tunes such as *Rhythm a Dim, Tumbling, I'm Thinking, Horse Power, The Lizard of Odds, Overweight and Underpaid, Riff Off, Not Yet, You First* and *Red Star* all have diminished scales in the melodies.

UPPER STRUCTURE TRIADS

Triads are three note chords of which there are five common types, major, minor, diminished, augmented and sus4. There are two types of upper structure triads, diatonic and non diatonic. The diatonic triads are from the chord scale while the non diatonic triads are usually borrowed from another scale or chromatic, neighboring tones.

For example, if you play an E♭ major triad over a G7 chord you are playing E♭ (♭13), G (1), B♭ (♯9). If you play an E♭ sus4 triad over G7 it gives you E♭ (♭13), A♭ (♭9), B♭ (♯9). In both instances it causes the chord to sound altered. If you play E major over G7 you are playing E (13), G♯ (♭9), B (3) which implies the sound of half step/whole step, symmetric diminished.

To hear all the possibilities it helps to go to a piano and play all five types of triads over the same bass note going up chromatically. Play all the major triads over C, i.e. C/C, D♭/C, D/C, E♭/C, E/C etc. Then do all the minor, diminished, augmented and sus4 triads. After examining the structures and their sound play triad over triad chromatically.

The bridges of *Stress Test, I'm Thinking* (improvised) and *Tumbling* are good examples of upper structure triads. Look for them in other tunes. You will hear them.

SYMMETRIC DIMINISHED SCALES

Both diminished scales consist of eight notes. Because of their symmetrical nature there are only three possible transpositions.

Example 1 | *Whole step/half step scale, 1st transposition*

Example 2 | *Whole step/half step scale, 2nd transposition*

Example 3 | *Whole step/half step scale, 3rd transposition*

Examples 1a, 2a and 3a are the same scales with the half step/whole step configuration pointed out from the 2nd, 4th, 6th and 8th degree. Beginning on the root of a dominant seventh chord the half step/whole step scale yields a dominant 7 ♭9 ♯9 ♯11 ♮13 chord. Any or all of the tensions may be used melodically or in a voicing.

Example 1a | *Half step/whole step scale starting from second degree of a whole step/half step scale*

Example 2a | *Half step/whole step scale, 2nd transposition*

Example 3a | *Half step/whole step scale, 3rd transposition*

Triads from the Half step/Whole step Diminished Scale

Example 1 | *Major triads*

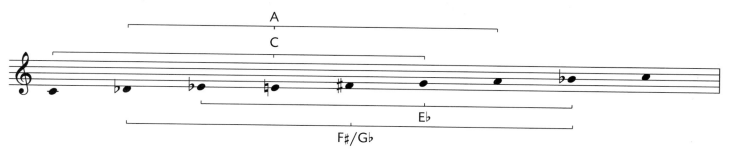

Example 2 | *Minor triads*

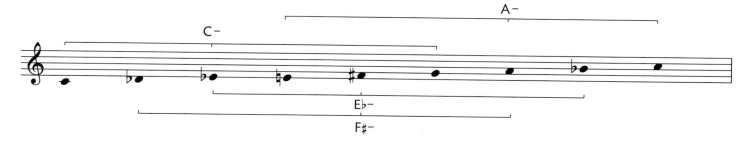

Sixth and Seventh Chords

Example 1 | *Minor seventh chords*

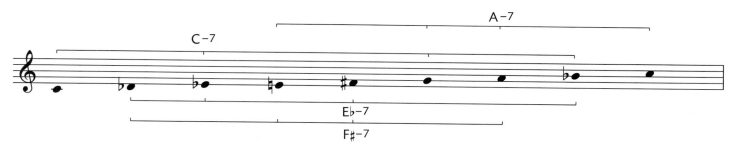

Example 2 | *Sixth and seventh chords (major, minor, half-diminished and diminished)*

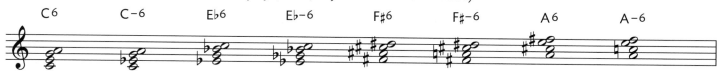

Example 3 | *Possible options for a dominant seventh chord*

Melodic Ideas from Arpeggios

Example 1 | *Combination of seventh chords and triads*

Example 2 | *Triads with ♭9*

Example 3 | *Inverted triads with #9*

Example 4 | *Inverted triads with #4*

Example 5 | *Inverted triads with #9 and ♭9*

Typical Diminished Ideas

Example 1 | *Intervalic patterns*

Fourths from the Half step/Whole step Diminished Scale

Example 1 | *Starting on different notes in the line will change its inflection*

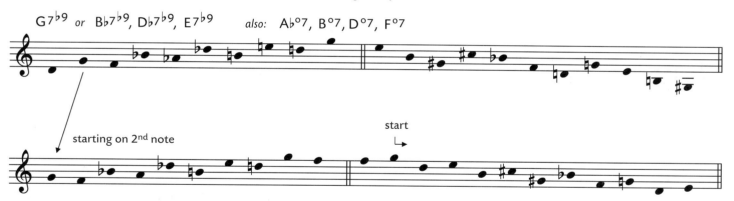

Example 2 | *2nd inversion triads yield sixths and fourths*

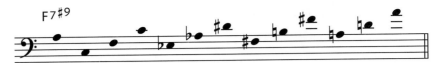

Example 3 | *Fourths and half steps*

Example 4 | *Fourths, half steps (2nd inversion triads)*

Melodic Study Over B Section Changes

Symmetric diminished scales over the dominant chords of the bridge can often imply other chords. In bar 3 there is an E major triad over G7, a G♭ major triad over C7 in bar 6 and a D major triad over F7 in bar 8.

Example 1

UPPER STRUCTURE TRIADS

Example 1 | *Upper structure triads in the tensions of scale chords*

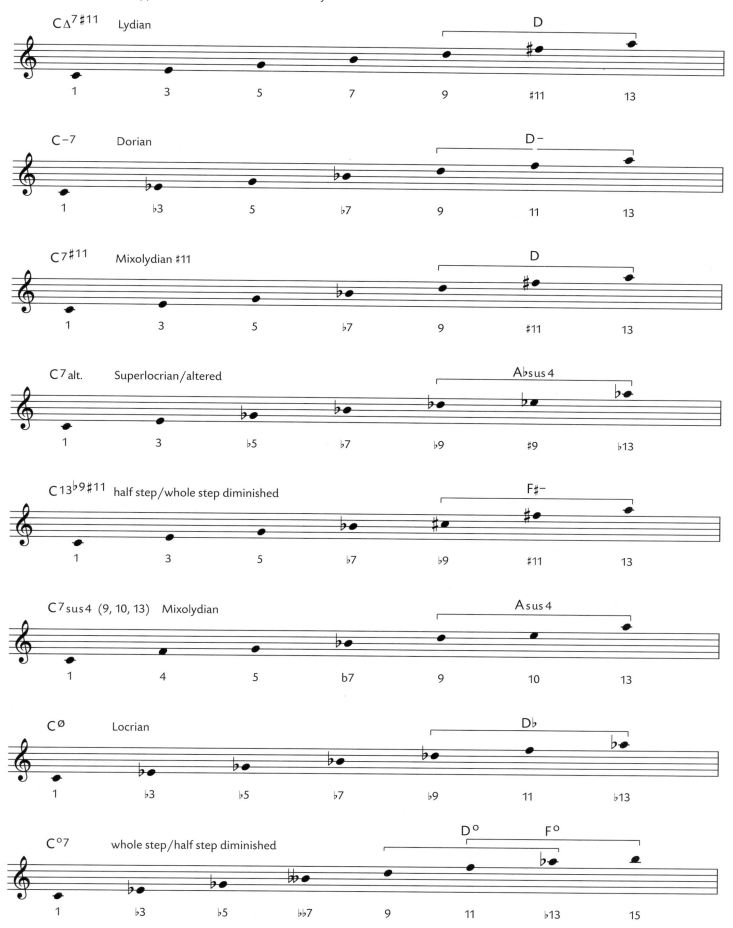

Tensions Available for Melodic Use Above Chords

Chord Type	Chord Tones	Tensions
Δ7	1, 3, 5, 7	9, #11, 13
Δ7♭5	1, 3, ♭5, 7	9, 13
Δ7#5	1, 3, #5, 7	9, #11, 13
–7	1, ♭3, 5, ♭7	9, 11, 13
o7	1, ♭3, ♭5, ♭♭7	9, 11, ♭13, 15
ø7 (–7♭5)	1, ♭3, ♭5, ♭7	♭9, 11, ♭13
ø♮9	1, ♭3, ♭5, ♭7	9, 11, ♭13
Δ6	1, 3, 5, 6	7, 9, #11
–6	1, ♭3, 5, 6	7, 9, 11
–Δ7	1, ♭3, 5, 7	9, 11, 13
Dominant 7	1, 3, 5, ♭7	9, 13
Dom. 7 #11	1, 3, 5, ♭7	9, #11, 13
Dom. 7 #5 (augmented)	1, 3, #5, ♭7	9, #11
Dom. 7sus4	1, 4, 5, ♭7	9, 10, 13
Dom. 7 ♭9	1, 3, 5, ♭7	♭9, #9, ♭13
Dom. 7 ♭9 ♮13	1, 3, 5, ♭7	♭9, #9, #11, 13
Dom. 7 altered	1, 3, ♭5, ♭7	♭9, #9, ♭13
Dom. 7 ♭5	1, 3, ♭5, ♭7	9, 13

Many more variations are possible, particularly with dominants.

Inversion Formulas

When inverting sixth and seventh chords it is useful to rotate the tensions (options) for that particular chord in their own cycles. After each inversion move to the nearest available tension.

Example 2 | *Δ7, –7, dominant 7, Lydian ♭7, ø7, –Δ7*

Root position	1, 3, 5, 7, 9, 11, 13
1st inversion	3, 5, 7, 1, 9, 11, 13
2nd inversion	5, 7, 1, 3, 11, 13, 9
3rd inversion	7, 1, 3, 5, 13, 9, 11

Example 3 | *Augmented 7, augmented Δ7*

Root position	1, 3, 5, 7, 9, 11
1st inversion	3, 5, 7, 1, 9, 11
2nd inversion	5, 7, 1, 3, 11, 9
3rd inversion	7, 1, 3, 5, 9, 11

Example 4 | *6, –6*

Root position	1, 3, 5, 6, 7, 9, 11
1st inversion	3, 5, 6, 7, 1, 9, 11
2nd inversion	5, 6, 1, 3, 11, 7, 9
3rd inversion	6, 1, 3, 5, 7, 9, 11

Example 5 | °7

Root position	1, 3, 5, 7, 9, 11, 13, 15 (Δ7)
1st inversion	3, 5, 7, 1, 9, 11, 13, 15
2nd inversion	5, 7, 1, 3, 11, 13, 15, 9
3rd inversion	7, 1, 3, 5, 13, 15, 9, 11

Example 6 | *Altered dominant 7*

Root position	1, 3, ♭5, ♭7, ♭9, ♯9, ♭13
1st inversion	3, ♭5, ♭7, 1, ♭9, ♯9, ♭13
2nd inversion	♭5, ♭7, 1, 3, ♭13, ♭9, ♯9
3rd inversion	♭7, 1, 3, ♭5, ♭13, ♭9, ♯9

Example 7 | *Dominant 7sus4*

Root position	1, 4, 5, ♭7, 9, 10, 13
1st inversion	4, 5, ♭7, 1, 9, 10, 13
2nd inversion	5, ♭7, 1, 4, 13, 9, 10
3rd inversion	♭7, 1, 4, 5, 13, 9, 10

Arpeggio Study with Tensions

After inverting each chord go to the nearest available tension. Inversions may start an octave lower.

Example 8 | *Inversion Formulas*

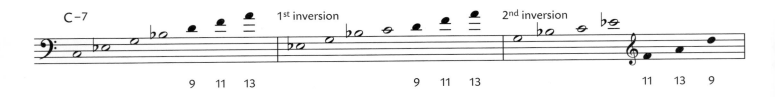

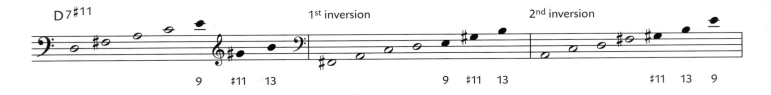

Adding approach notes to the chord tones can produce interesting melodies.

Example 9 | *Approach notes*

Melodic Study Over B Section Changes

Upper structure triads can be taken from different chord scales: diminished, Lydian ♭7, Mixolydian and even totally non-related.

Example 1

I'M THINKING

Bruce Gertz

I'M THINKING

C concert

Bruce Gertz

THE LIZARD OF ODDS

Drums and bass play 8 bars intro on track 21 (slow).

Bruce Gertz

THE LIZARD OF ODDS
Drums and bass play 8 bars intro on track 21 (slow).

C concert

Bruce Gertz

RHYTHM A DIM

A sections are all Bb7 Funk/Hip Hop.
B section is swing with chord changes.

Bruce Gertz

Disc **2**
Track 23
or
Disc 1
Track 15

bass

Funk Bb7

Bb7

swing F–7   Bb7   Eb7

C7   F7

Funk Bb7

RHYTHM A DIM

All the **A** sections are B♭7 Funk/Hip Hop
and the **B** section is swing with chord changes.

Bruce Gertz

STRESS TEST
(1st part)

Bruce Gertz

Disc **2**
Track 24

bass

tacet (rhythm only)

STRESS TEST
(2nd part)

Bruce Gertz

STRESS TEST
(1st part)

Bruce Gertz

Disc **2**
Track 24

C concert

tacet (rhythm only)

STRESS TEST
(2nd part)

Bruce Gertz

tacet (rhythm only)

RING AROUND URANUS

Bruce Gertz

Disc **2**
Track 25
or
Disc 1
Track 19

RING AROUND URANUS

C concert

Bruce Gertz

DIRTY DETAILS

Bruce Gertz

Disc **2**
Track 26
Track 27
(F pedal)

bass

F (dominant) pedal (16 bars, track 27 only)

(F pedal)

F (dominant) pedal (8 bars, track 27 only)

DIRTY DETAILS

C concert

Bruce Gertz

HORSE POWER

Bruce Gertz

HORSE POWER

C concert

Bruce Gertz

TUMBLING

Disc **2**
Track 29

Bruce Gertz

TUMBLING

C concert

Bruce Gertz

INTERVALIC MELODIES

There are two types of intervalic melodies: diatonic and non-diatonic. A diatonic intervalic melody is one which uses the intervals from the relative scale. If you play up a third, down a step, up a fifth etc. each of those intervals would be deemed major, minor, diminished, augmented or perfect depending upon the scale. In the case of a non-diatonic intervalic melody you may set up a scheme which maintains the same type of intervals regardless of any scale. One example would be up a major third, down a half step, up a perfect fourth and down a half step then start again. You could play it backwards, retrograde, inverted or both.

Intervalic melodies are often the most interesting because they can be in and out at the same time and may not sound as typical as a chord or scale idea. Once you have a starting note the choices are to move up or down by any interval within playing range be it small or large. Naturally some large intervals such as a 23rd or greater may not be playable at a fast tempo while notes within an octave or two could be. There is a symmetry in non-diatonic interval structures that allow lines to resolve when they complete a cycle. The following are some examples of intervalic melodies: *Quarts and Fifths* and *Red Note Special.* See if you can find the intervalic ideas.

To go deeper into this type of playing there is a book which I highly recommend, entitled *Thesaurus of Intervalic Melodies* by Jerry Bergonzi (advance music no. 14265). There are over 1700 intervalic melodies in the book followed by intervalic tunes.

When improvising over a tune practice maintaining awareness of the chord changes while playing intervalically against them. Some of the notes may be in and some may be out. Notice the tonal colors as you move between the in and out sounds. The structure of your intervalic melody should be strong enough to stand on its own and this is one reason for it to work.

INTERVALIC LINES

**Example 1 | ** *Major triads moving up in whole steps*

It is a good exercise to change the sequence of notes in an arpeggio: 1357, 1375, 1735, 1753, and so on. Including the inversions there are 24 permutations for a seventh chord. The next example combines two sequences (1375 and 3157) over major seventh chords to form an intervalic line in ascending major thirds. The notes come from the hexatonic (six-note) symmetric augmented scale.

**Example 2 | ** *Major seventh chord sequence*

Example 3

Example 4

Example 5

**Example 6 | ** *Whole step/half step symmetric diminished scale*

Example 7

Example 8

↑P4 ↓m2 ↑P4 ↓P5

Example 9 | *Symmetric augmented scale*

↑P5 ↓m3 ↑P5 ↓m3

symmetric augmented scale (hexatonic)

Example 10

↓m2 ↑P4 ↓m2 ↓M3

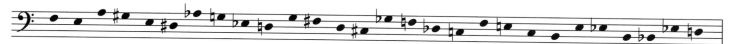

Example 11 | *7sus4 chords ascending in major thirds*

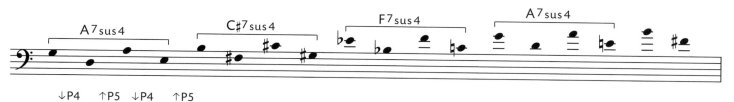

↓P4   ↑P5   ↓P4   ↑P5

Example 12 | *Interlocking inverted seventh chords in ascending major seconds. The root of one chord becomes the*
♭7 of the next. This is called a "pivot tone".

↑M6 ↓m3 ↓M3

Legend: ↑ = up, ↓ = down, m = minor, M = major, P = perfect

Melodic Study Over B Section Changes
Intervalic lines using 2nds, 5ths, 4ths in the first 4 bars then movin to 6ths in the last 4 bars.

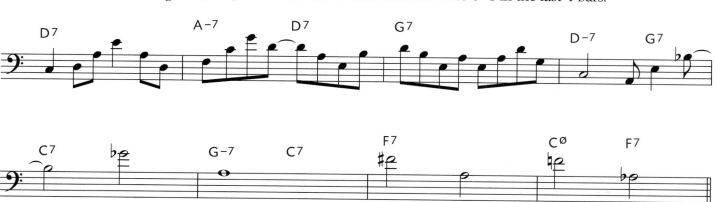

QUARTS & FIFTHS

F dominant pedal on **A** sections, chord changes at **B**.

Bruce Gertz

QUARTS & FIFTHS

F dominant pedal on **A** sections, chord changes at **B**.

C concert

Bruce Gertz

F (dominant) pedal (16 bars)

play changes

F (dominant) pedal (8 bars)

RED NOTE SPECIAL

Disc **2**
Track 31

bass

Bruce Gertz

RED NOTE SPECIAL

C concert

Bruce Gertz

ABOUT THE AUTHOR

BIOGRAPHY

American, acoustic and electric bass player and composer, born in Providence, Rhode Island.

Bruce Gertz began playing guitar at the age of ten. By age fourteen he changed to the bass guitar and started playing rock, blues and later jazz. While attending Berklee College of Music in Boston as a composition and arranging major, Bruce studied acoustic bass under John Neves and William Curtis.

He began freelancing in the Boston area and soon built a reputation as a versatile player and soloist on both acoustic and electric bass. Gertz became associated with Bill Frisell, Mick Goodrick, Mike Stern, George Garzone, Jerry Bergonzi and other top players in Boston through time.

Later Bruce studied more advanced jazz improvisation with Charlie Banacos and also through association with Jerry Bergonzi.

Bruce has also toured with Billy Eckstine, Maynard Ferguson, Marlena Shaw, Gary Burton, Dave Brubeck, Jerry Bergonzi and others.

More about Bruce Gertz on **www.brucegertz.com.**

Awards
- 1987 Boston Music Awards – "Outstanding Bassist"
- 1988 Boston Music Awards – "Outstanding Bassist"
- 1990 Boston Music Awards – "Outstanding Bassist"
- 1991 Boston Music Awards – "Outstanding Bassist"
- 1992 Billboard Song Contest – Third Prize for the song "Blueprint"
- 1992 National Endowment for the Arts. "Jazz Performance Grant"
- 1993 the album "Blueprint" (Evidence Music ECD 22196-2)
- 1995 the album "Third Eye" (Ram Records RMCD 4509)
- 1996 the album "Discovery Zone" (Ram Records RMCD 4524)
- 1997 the album "Blueprint" (Evidence Music) all nominated for "Outstanding Jazz"
- 1997 Composition Grant, Massachusetts Cultural Council
- 1999 the album "Red Handed" – "Outstanding Jazz CD"
- 2001 the album "The Line Between" – "Outstanding Jazz CD"
- 2003 the album "Dreaming Out Loud" – "Outstanding Jazz CD"

PERFORMANCE EXPERIENCE

Being an established performer in New England, Bruce has accompanied many well known jazz artists: Gil Evans, Danilo Perez, Junior Cook, Dave Brubeck, Bob Berg, Mike Stern, Charles McPherson, George Cables, Diane Schurr, Bobby Tucker, Tom Harrell, Joe Lovano, Bill Frisell, Lee Konitz, Jon Hendricks, Cab Calloway, Joe Williams, Oliver Lake, Mark Murphy, George Coleman, John Abercrombie, Gary Burton, George Garzone, Tim Hagans, Kenny Werner, Billy Hart, Mick Goodrick, Pat Metheny, Ted Curson, Eddie Harris, Eric Kloss, The Fifth Dimension, Freddie Cole, Donald Byrd, Charlie Byrd, Joey Calderazzo, Cyrus Chestnut, Aaron Goldberg, Larry Goldings and Cecil Payne are some of these artists.
Bruce has also toured with Billy Eckstine, Maynard Ferguson, Marlena Shaw, Gary Burton, Dave Brubeck, Jerry Bergonzi and others.

TEACHING EXPERIENCE

- 1974 – present: private instructor
- 1976 – present: professor at Berklee College of Music, Boston
- 1985 – present: Bruce has taught workshops with Berklee in Japan, Spain, Germany, Italy and Santa Cruz de Tenerife and as a leader or with Jerry Bergonzi in Australia and the U.S.

SELECTED DISCOGRAPHY

Blueprint – Evidence Music ECD 22196-2
Third Eye – Ram Records RMCD4509
Sunscreams – Ram Records RMCD4507
Discovery Zone – Ram Records, RMCD4524
Shut Wide Open – Doubletime Records DTRCD 132
Simple Pleasures – Ram Records RMCD4525
Red Handed – Doubletime Records DTRCD 155
The Line Between – Whaling City Sound WCS 009
The Good Listener – Ram Records RMCD4510
Dreaming Out Loud – Whaling City Sound WCS 020

PUBLICATIONS

Mastering the Bass Book 1, Mel Bay Publications
Mastering the Bass (series), Mel Bay Publications
Walkin, Bruce Gertz Music
22 Contemporary Melodic Studies for Electric Bass Vol. 1, Bruce Gertz Music MB -1

Instructional videos
Walkin, Bruce Gertz Music WV -1

Articles
Harmonizing a Melody, Bass Player Magazine March, 1993
Triad Twister, Bass Player Magazine, Fall 1999

Instructional CD
Jazz Workshop for Bass and Drums, with Dave Weigert, advance music 14601, 1996

Bruce Gertz

LET'S PLAY RHYTHM

Play-Along 1

(Rhythm Section only)

BROADCASTING PROHIBITED. ALLE URHEBER- UND LEISTUNGSSCHUTZRECHTE VORBEHALTEN. KEIN VERLEIH! KEINE UNERLAUBTE VERVIELFÄLTIGUNG, VERMIETUNG, AUFFÜHRUNG, SENDUNG! ALL RIGHTS RESERVED. UNAUTHORIZED COPYING, REPRODUCTION, HIRING, LENDING, PUBLIC PERFORMANCE AND

GEMA

COMPACT disc DIGITAL AUDIO DDD

LC 01647

14272-1

1

© 2005 advance music
℗ 2005 advance music

Bruce Gertz

LET'S PLAY RHYTHM

Play-Along 2

(Rhythm Section and Melodies)

BROADCASTING PROHIBITED. ALLE URHEBER- UND LEISTUNGSSCHUTZRECHTE VORBEHALTEN. KEIN VERLEIH! KEINE UNERLAUBTE VERVIELFÄLTIGUNG, VERMIETUNG, AUFFÜHRUNG, SENDUNG! ALL RIGHTS RESERVED. UNAUTHORIZED COPYING, REPRODUCTION, HIRING, LENDING, PUBLIC PERFORMANCE AND

GEMA

COMPACT disc DIGITAL AUDIO DDD

LC 01647

14272-2

2

© 2005 advance music
℗ 2005 advance music

Bruce Gertz

LET'S PLAY RHYTHM

Listening Version

GEMA

compact disc DIGITAL AUDIO DDD

LC 01647

14272-3

3

© 2005 advance music
℗ 2005 advance music

ALLE URHEBER- UND LEISTUNGSSCHUTZRECHTE VORBEHALTEN. KEIN VERLEIH! KEINE UNERLAUBTE VERVIELFÄLTIGUNG, VERMIETUNG, AUFFÜHRUNG, SENDUNG! ALL RIGHTS RESERVED. UNAUTHORIZED COPYING, REPRODUCTION, HIRING, LENDING, PUBLIC PERFORMANCE AND BROADCASTING PROHIBITED.